Danny Elfman's Batman in Focus

by
Mark Wilderspin

Rhinegold Publishing Ltd
241 Shaftesbury Avenue
London WC2H 8TF
Telephone: 020 7333 1720
Fax: 020 7333 1765
www.rhinegold.co.uk

Also available from Rhinegold Publishing:
Madonna: *The Immaculate Collection* in Focus
The Who: *Who's Next* in Focus
John Barry's *Goldfinger* in Focus
Baroque Music in Focus
Modernism in Focus
Romanticism in Focus
Musicals in Focus
A Student's Guide to Music Technology for the Edexcel AS and A2 Specification
Listening Tests for Students for the Edexcel AS and A2 Specification

Rhinegold Music Study Guides
(series editor: Paul Terry)
A Student's Guide to Music Technology for the Edexcel AS and A2 Specifications
Listening Tests for Students for the Edexcel AS and A2 Music Technology Specifications
Students' Guides to GCSE, AS and A2 Music for the AQA, Edexcel and OCR Specifications
Listening Tests for GCSE, AS and A2 Music for the AQA, Edexcel and OCR Specifications
A Student's Guide to GCSE Music for the WJEC Specification

Key Stage 3 Elements
Key Stage 3 Listening Tests: Books 1 and 2
Music Literacy Workbook (for GCSE and A-level)
A Student's Guide to Harmony and Counterpoint (for AS and A2 Music)

Rhinegold Education also publishes Classroom Music, Teaching Drama, Rhinegold Dictionary of Music in Sound, Rhinegold Guide to Music Education, and study guides for Classical Civilisation, Drama and Theatre Studies, Performance Studies and Religious Studies.

First published in 2007, new edition in 2008 in Great Britain by
Rhinegold Publishing Ltd
241 Shaftesbury Avenue
London WC2H 8TF
Telephone: 020 7333 1720
Fax: 020 7333 1765
www.rhinegold.co.uk
© Rhinegold Publishing Ltd 2007, 2008

You should always check the current requirements of the examination, since these may change. Copies of the Edexcel Specification may be obtained from Edexcel Examinations at Edexcel Publications, Adamsway, Mansfield, Nottinghamshire, NG18 4FN Telephone: 01623 467467, Fax 01623 450481, Email publications@linneydirect.com See also the Edexcel website at www.edexcel.org.uk

Mark Wilderspin: Batman in Focus
British Library Cataloguing in Publication Data.
A catalogue record for this book is available from the British Library.
ISBN: 978-1-906178-58-1
Printed in Great Britain by Headley Brothers Ltd

Contents

The author

Mark Wilderspin is Head of Curricular Music at St Paul's Girls' School in Hammersmith, having taught previously at Queenswood School, Hatfield (where he was Composer in Residence), Fulham Prep School and the Junior Department of the Royal College of Music in London. For Rhinegold Publishing he was a co-author for *KS3 Elements*. As a composer he specialises in music for film and multimedia, with recent clients including Historic Royal Palaces, eMoot, BBC R&D and *The World of Beatrix Potter* attraction. He has also worked closely with film composer Trevor Jones as a programmer and arranger on a number of Hollywood feature films.

Acknowledgements

Mark Wilderspin would like to thank Sheryl Morgan, David Ventura and Lucien Jenkins for their support and assistance during the preparation of this book.

Thanks also to Sarah Smith, Elisabeth Boulton, Ben Robbins, Emma Findlow, Chris Elcombe, Hallam Bannister and Sabine Wolf of Rhinegold Publishing for their assistance throughout the editing and production process.

Copyright acknowledgements

1
Introduction and background

Introduction

Danny Elfman is well known today as a film and television composer. Even if his name is not too familiar, his work should be: he is the composer of the themes to *The Simpsons* and *Desperate Housewives*, of the music for (among many others) *Charlie and the Chocolate Factory, Good Will Hunting, Sleepy Hollow, Men in Black, Spider-Man, Hulk* and Tim Burton's two *Batman* films, of which this book examines the first (made in 1989) in detail.

> For a detailed list of Elfman's film and TV work, his listing on IMDB (the Internet Movie Database) is a good place to start: www.imdb.com His unofficial fansite 'Music for a darkened people' may also be a useful reference point: http://elfman.filmmusic.com

It is Danny Elfman's score for *Batman* which really launched him into the mainstream and amongst the top-flight Hollywood film composers. It was a similar turning point for the film's director and long-time collaborator, Tim Burton. Elfman had worked with Burton before (on *Pee-wee's Big Adventure* and *Beetlejuice*, for example), but this was the first time either of them had been hired to do a major summer blockbuster. The bigger budgets inherent in this led to a substantial score of some 80 minutes, for large orchestra (and occasional use of choir) coupled with extra synth and sampled lines added by Elfman. It is still one of the best known of Elfman's scores and shows a great deal of the stylistic traits and influences that were to pervade his later work, as well as inspiring other composers.

The film was a commercial success for Warner Brothers, due in no small part to some well-timed hype and an aggressive marketing strategy for the film and its associated products. In addition to grossing over $413,000,000 (£209,300,000) worldwide, it received the Oscar for Best Art Direction-Set Decoration in 1990 and remains the best known and most commercially successful *Batman* film.

Elfman's background and early career

Danny Elfman was born in 1953 in California and from an early age was interested in films, though at high school he wanted to be a film-maker rather than a film composer. Elfman did not go to university after leaving school, choosing instead to follow his brother Richard Elfman (a film-maker) to Paris and play in a music troupe there. He then went travelling around Africa, which brought him into contact with a wide variety of unusual ethnic instruments, particularly percussion instruments.

> To this day, Elfman's music has a fascination with rhythm and percussive timbres, many of which are actually laid down by Elfman himself as pre-recorded tracks (whether samples or played live) on the film score.

Returning to California, Elfman's interest in composition arose from co-founding (with his brother) the *Mystic Knights of Oingo Boingo*. This was essentially an experimental cabaret act which later became the rock band *Oingo Boingo*. The group performed the soundtrack for Richard Elfman's first feature film, *The Forbidden Zone*, in 1978.

Tim Burton was such a fan of *Oingo Boingo* that he invited Danny Elfman to compose the score for *Pee-wee's Big Adventure* (1985). This was Elfman's first orchestral score, though he had composed a concerto for piano and ensemble (the *Oingo Boingo Piano Concerto One and a Half*) while a member of the *Mystic Knights*. Despite being initially apprehensive, Elfman was persuaded to work on the project, enlisting the help of fellow *Oingo Boingo* band member Steve Bartek, who acted as arranger and orchestrator. The success of this collaboration led to Elfman scoring Burton's *Beetlejuice* (1988, in which some of the stylistic traits that were to be amplified and refined in later scores are already evident) and, the following year, to working on *Batman*.

To date, Burton has worked with Elfman on 11 films, from *Pee-Wee's Big Adventure* to *Corpse Bride* (2005). Elfman also contributed the theme (but not the score) to Burton's *The World of Stainboy* in 2000. For both composer and director, these collaborations form the bulk of their output.

Style and context of Burton's Batman

Burton is known as a director with a penchant for black comedy, witnessed by such films as *Beetlejuice, Edward Scissorhands, Sleepy Hollow* and *Corpse Bride*. The dark tone and gothic elements are crucial to the 1989 *Batman* film (and are even more pronounced in the 1992 sequel, *Batman Returns*). From the enormous gothic cathedral used as the setting for the film's conclusion to the gloomy innards of the Batcave, the locations and scenery within the film uphold the dark tone set by Burton. The majority of the film is also set at night, seemingly the only time that the caped crusader operates. Even the few daytime scenes are filmed in gloomy and overcast weather. This could not be in sharper contrast to the lurid colours of the 1960s *Batman* television series, which, along with the 1966 feature film spin-off, was the previous screen incarnation. Burton's *Batman* is a brooding, grittier hero, who takes to fighting street crime because his own parents died as a result of it. He operates outside the law and has an ambiguous relationship with the public, once his existence is known: is he friend or foe?

> Burton's more recent 'reimaginings' are similarly darker in tone and style to their predecessors. See *Planet of the Apes* (2001) and *Charlie and the Chocolate Factory* (2005), both also scored by Elfman.

The film's set design and costume give slightly contradictory senses of chronology. The Gotham skyline seems almost futuristic, yet the costume and interiors of the journalists and newspaper offices suggest the 1930s or 1940s. This latter point, coupled with the numerous nocturnal scenes, gives *Batman* the feel of a classic film noir. It is only the songs from Prince's contemporary soundtrack that provide the film with any firm indication of originating in the late 1980s.

Characters

Bruce Wayne/Batman	Millionaire Bruce Wayne has inherited his fortune from his parents, who were murdered when he was a child. By night he assumes the alter ego of Batman, a vigilante who dresses in an armour-plated bat costume and uses a combination of intense physical training and high-tech gadgets to fight crime.
Jack Napier/Joker	Jack Napier is Carl Grissom's right-hand man. A hardened criminal with psychotic tendencies, he harbours ambitions of succeeding Grissom and is secretly having an affair with his mistress. After falling into a vat of acid at Axis Chemicals, he is physically disfigured and reinvents himself as the Joker. The transformation seems to intensify his psychotic behaviour and to broaden his ambitions; he sets himself up in opposition to Batman and attempts to take control of the city.
Alexander Knox	A local reporter who has an obsession with the Batman story and, despite ridicule by colleagues who don't believe the story, persists in trying to find out more from the police, with little success.
Lieutenant Eckhardt	A corrupt police officer who is on Grissom's payroll. He has a strong dislike for both Knox and Napier, eventually being shot by the latter at Axis Chemicals.
Mayor Borg	An old and incompetent mayor who has pinned everything on Commissioner Gordon and Harvey Dent solving his city's problems.
Commissioner Gordon	The chief of police who is trying to work with Harvey Dent to uproot crime and corruption in the city. He is cautious about Batman's allegiances.
Harvey Dent	Newly-appointed district attorney for Gotham City. Although he has been given responsibility for cleaning up the city, he is rendered largely superfluous by Batman's interventions.
Alicia	Grissom's mistress and eventually the Joker's girlfriend. The Joker disfigures her as an 'artistic experiment' and she commits suicide.
Vicki Vale	A beautiful photo-journalist who arrives in Gotham to cover the Batman story. She befriends Alexander Knox and falls for Bruce Wayne, though the Joker also has an interest in her.
Carl Grissom	An old but tough crime magnate who presides over an empire that is running Gotham City into the ground. He knows that Jack Napier is not as trustworthy as he seems and deliberately informs the police (via Lieutenant Eckhardt) of Napier's operation to clear traces of criminal activity at Axis Chemicals. Grissom is ultimately murdered by Napier after the latter becomes the Joker.
Alfred	Bruce Wayne's long-serving butler. Alfred alone knows Bruce's secret identity.
Bob	Faithful sidekick of Jack Napier (and, subsequently, Napier as the Joker).

Synopsis

Gotham City is trying to mount a festival to celebrate its 200th anniversary, but is gripped by a crime syndicate run by Carl Grissom. Trade has slumped, the festival is massively in debt and, despite the best efforts of Mayor Borg in appointing Harvey Dent as the new district attorney, the city is being run into the ground by crime. There are murmurs of a mysterious vigilante who calls himself 'Batman' and stalks criminals at night. Although the story will not be confirmed by police, it has become a minor obsession for local reporter Alexander Knox and photo-journalist Vicki Vale, who has come to Gotham to find out more.

Batman pounces on some muggers at night, telling them who he is and that they should warn all their friends. Meanwhile, Harvey Dent has learned that Carl Grissom is using Axis Chemicals as a front company for his underworld organisation. Grissom sends Jack Napier to destroy the company's records, then tips off the police to apprehend him as he knows that Napier is secretly having an affair with his mistress, Alicia.

Millionaire Bruce Wayne hosts a charity fundraiser for the festival at his home, Wayne Manor. Vicki Vale and Alexander Knox attend to try and find out more about Batman from police commissioner Gordon, but both he and Harvey Dent deny any knowledge. Commissioner Gordon learns of the Axis arrest and goes to oversee the operation. Bruce Wayne also learns of this and goes as Batman to intervene. There he confronts Napier and in the course of a struggle, Napier falls into a vat of acid, though he amazingly survives. Batman escapes before the police can apprehend him, but now there can be no doubt of the rumours.

Vicki and Bruce have dinner at Wayne Manor. Jack Napier has surgery to try and repair the severed nerves in his face where he was hit by a bullet, but is left with a permanent sardonic grin. Moreover, the chemicals have bleached his skin white and turned his hair green, lending him the appearance of a demonic circus clown. Adopting the name Joker, he seeks out Grissom and murders him in revenge for setting him up.

The morning after having dinner with Vicki, Bruce claims he can't see her because he needs to go away on business, but when it seems that his Butler Alfred knows nothing of this, Vicki is curious and follows Bruce as he stays in Gotham to lay flowers in a back alley. As Vicki tries to work out the mystery behind Bruce Wayne, the Joker takes over Grissom's affairs, killing any former associates who get in his way.

The Joker carries out a plan to terrorise Gotham City by tainting a number of cosmetics with the components of Smilex, a chemical that kills instantly when mixed, leaving the victim with a permanent grin just like the Joker's. This leaves the city in turmoil as citizens try to work out what to make of Batman and the mysterious 'Joker' who has claimed responsibility for the crime.

The Joker, who has decided that he wants Vicki for himself, invites her to the museum by pretending to be Bruce Wayne, though she is rescued by Batman after the Joker has gone around defacing and destroying works of art in the museum. After escaping in the Batmobile, Batman takes Vicki back to the Batcave and reveals that he has cracked the Joker's poison code. He tells Vicki to take the information to the press.

The next day, Bruce goes to Vicki's apartment to apologise for his erratic behaviour and attempts to explain that he is Batman. Meanwhile, the Joker has also decided to see Vicki at her apartment and shoots Bruce, who nevertheless escapes having used a silver tray to stop the bullet. Vicki later finds out that Bruce's parents were murdered in the alley where she saw him lay flowers.

The Joker goes on television to say that he is going to the festival to release $20 million in cash on the crowd. He also challenges Batman to show up for a final confrontation.

When Bruce realises it was the Joker (as Jack Napier) who killed his parents years before, Alfred brings Vicki into the Batcave. After a reconciliation between the two of them, Batman uses the Batmobile to blow up Axis Chemicals and prepares for a final showdown with the Joker at the anniversary festival celebrations. The Joker shoots Batman down as he attacks in the Batwing (an airborne version of the Batmobile) and heads for the cathedral to make his escape with Vicki. Batman survives to pursue them to the top, where the Joker eventually falls to his doom. Batman finds his place within society, vowing to protect the city and work with the police (hence his bequest of the Bat-signal to call him). He has also avenged the death of his parents and can move on in his relationship with Vicki.

2
Into the music

The sound of Elfman's score

Danny Elfman's score for *Batman* is a tour de force of orchestral underscore, musical effects and characterisation. Although undoubtedly the most memorable music in the score is that derived from the initial five-note 'Bat-theme' (see page 14), Elfman uses a lot of other material besides this for specific functions: to characterise the Joker, to punctuate scene changes and to provide a diegetic underscore for items such as the Joker's commercial for Smilex products. Moreover, Elfman's music is not the only music heard in the movie: there are arrangements of the popular song *Beautiful Dreamer* (words and music by Stephen Foster), an arrangement of part of Max Steiner's theme to *A Summer Place* (1959), and songs written and performed by Prince. These three are all examples of music which is appropriated by the character of the Joker within the film, insofar as there is no real 'Joker-theme' in the score. Instead, Elfman provides the Joker with a number of styles of music, including a Viennese-style waltz tune and music using whole-tone textures.

There are two soundtrack albums for *Batman* available: one containing songs written and performed by Prince (labelled as the 'Motion Picture Soundtrack' and with the movie's iconic Bat-emblem on the front cover) and one with a selection of music from the original score (with a smaller Bat-emblem as a silhouette in front of the moon and described as the 'Motion Picture Score'). Only the second album contains Elfman's music.

> Both albums are released by Warner Brothers: The Prince album is catalogue number 7599-35936-2; the album containing Elfman's music has catalogue number 7599-25977-2. The Prince album and its relationship with the score are discussed on page 21.

Elfman's working methods

Although music technology has moved on considerably since 1989, Danny Elfman's music for *Batman* was created in a similar way to most contemporary film scores. An outline of the process may be crudely summarised as follows:

> By 1989, the MIDI protocol that had been introduced six years earlier was the main way of controlling and communicating with synthesisers and newly-developed samplers. Elfman has been a keen follower of the latest technological trends and has kept pace with them over the years.

- The composer works on a specific cue, having obtained precise timings and discussed which features of the cue should be highlighted and whether there are any sync points

- A sequencer is used to create a tempo map, to record musical ideas and to develop a 'sketch' or demo of the cue that can be played against the picture. This is usually shown to the director for approval. Some of the tracks laid down at this stage (synth lines, pads, electronic percussion and some sampled instruments) will end up on the final score – they may be recorded separately as audio tracks at a later stage
- The sequencer data (MIDI file or score printout) is passed on to an orchestrator or arranger, normally with a recording of the 'sketch' of the cue. The orchestrator is then responsible for producing a full score of the cue, taking note of the instrumentation available and fleshing out the sketch to be a proper realisation of the music. The orchestrator will then often leave the generating and printing of parts to a copyist.

Although not all of the specific details of Elfman's process on *Batman* are known, we know from interviews and from reports at the time that Elfman was a user of MOTU's *Performer* sequencing software to control his hardware synthesisers and samplers. *Performer* was one of the earliest professional application programs designed for the Mac and first appeared in 1985. It enjoyed popularity among film composers and in 1990 was renamed *Digital Performer* once it began to incorporate the handling of digital audio within its interface. This latter incarnation of the software continues to be developed to this day.

Elfman worked with orchestrator Steve Bartek and two other orchestrators on *Batman*, and used the score printout function within *Performer* to provide them with the music for orchestration. As is common with most of Elfman's later scores, his strong leanings towards percussion meant that a lot of synthetic percussion tracks were recorded by him in *Performer*. These remain on the score, as well as various other synth tracks and sound design-type effects. The score is therefore more of an electro-acoustic hybrid than it might at first appear.

Shirley Walker and Steven Scott Smalley are credited on the album sleeve as contributing 'additional orchestrations'. Shirley Walker also conducted the score during recording.

As Elfman has pointed out in various interviews connected with a number of different scoring projects, he prefers to spend a couple of weeks in advance of working directly to picture, in order to generate thematic ideas for the film. Once the first working cut is available he will then select three large cues that he feels are central to the film: one from the beginning, middle and end of the film. Once these are in place, he reckons on having a refined pool of thematic material from which to work and the three main cues as reference points for developing the drama musically. In general, he then works chronologically through the remainder of the cues, keeping a close eye on the number of days left to complete the score and the number of minutes of music he must therefore compose each day. As in the three-point model above, a production line evolves, where Elfman finishes cues, which are passed on to Steve Bartek for orchestration, and then on to a copyist to generate parts. The whole process is enormously time-pressured: scores have to be written in anything from four to 12 weeks – with six weeks being the norm.

Common techniques: the Elfman 'sound'

Elfman's musical voice is now very familiar within Hollywood film scores, but near the beginning of his career he brought together a collection of styles and techniques that were not commonly found in film scores of the time. During the 1990s (as one of Hollywood's most in-demand composers), his style was emulated and pastiched widely, particularly the sound-world of *Edward Scissorhands* (1990). This score in many ways encapsulates some of the crucial elements of Elfman's style, and particularly fits the labels often bestowed upon his music ('dark', 'twisted', 'bittersweet'). It certainly demonstrates the uneasy marriage of gothic melancholy and wry humour that seems to pervade much of Elfman's work around this time. It is interesting that, when asked which of his scores Elfman is most proud of, *Edward Scissorhands* is still the answer most consistently given. It is clear that Elfman felt that he had really discovered a personal voice in that score, and its influence on *Batman Returns* two years later is quite striking.

> If Elfman's *Edward Scissorhands* is a score that spawned a number of emulations during the early- and mid-1990s, then a modern-day equivalent might be Thomas Newman's iconic score for *American Beauty* (1999), which has had a profound influence on the sound-world of modern film and television scores.

The following list goes some way to capturing the essence of Elfman's compositional techniques:

- Quirky melodic writing, often in a minor key and with a penchant for triple metre (or mixing sections in triple and quadruple metres)
- Cartoon-style 'mickey-mousing' and musical mimicking of gestures
- Use of the tritone (augmented 4th/diminished 5th), both melodically and harmonically
- Use of the whole-tone scale, both melodically and to form chords
- A 'cascading' figure (usually descending and most often played by violins), which is used as a comic or attention-grabbing gesture, such as the example below, based on the whole-tone scale
- Emphasis on percussion: cross-rhythms, layered ostinati, combinations of orchestral, real, sampled and synthesised percussion, often performed by Elfman himself.

'Cascading' strings idea

Fast

Furthermore, there are certain instrumental timbres and textures which are favoured by Elfman:

- Extreme low timbres: low strings, bassoon and contrabassoon, trombones, tuba, lowest octaves of the piano

- Extreme high timbres: celesta/music box, harp, string harmonics
- Vocal timbres, whether real or synthesised
- Synth layers and electronic percussion (a particularly strong feature since *Planet of the Apes* in 2001).

A cursory listen to any number of Elfman's film scores will reveal these and other common features. Of all of these, one needs special amplification. It is Elfman's use of the tritone in his compositions. The tritone (so called because it is an interval comprising three whole tones from the root note) is an interval which is not easily harmonised or used melodically. It has a quirkiness that is inherent in it being neither a perfect 4th nor a perfect 5th, though it can be used as a comic substitute for either. It is entirely suited to Elfman's sound world and there are countless examples of it within his work. Here is perhaps the most famous example:

Opening gesture of *The Simpsons* theme, by Danny Elfman

As is well known, the tune then goes on to adopt the tritone at the beginning of the ensuing faster section, but then as here it resolves upwards to the expected perfect 5th, treating the tritone as an appoggiatura (rather like the famous tune of 'Maria' in Bernstein's *West Side Story*). However, a more deep-rooted use of the tritone comes during the end credits of *The Simpsons*, where the following typically Elfmanesque bass line is found:

The Simpsons, end credits, bass line

These are both very melodic uses of the tritone, but Elfman also favours juxtaposing two chords a tritone apart. Here is an example from the main titles to *Spider-Man*:

Spider-Man, horn entry in the main titles

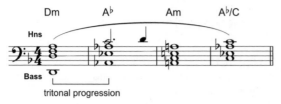

tritonal progression

Although chords a tritone apart are tonally just about as far removed from each other as possible, it is interesting that Elfman here moves immediately to a chord more closely related to the first chord (in others words, the A minor is far closer to D minor, as the dominant minor, than it is to the Ab chord in the middle of them both). In this way, Elfman almost negates the tonal implications of the troublesome Ab chord. In context, it seems therefore to be chosen more for its colour and sound than because it is useful for Elfman to modulate somewhere else. There is a parallel in *Batman* with the use of the sixth note (bracketed in the example below) of the Bat-theme. The note is usually harmonised with chord II (in the major mode) – thus a D major chord in C minor, and a C# major chord in the B minor of the opening titles. Immediately after the C# chord, the music picks up again faster in B minor as if nothing had happened, whereas an orthodox use of the chord might have been to modulate to the dominant (as C# is the dominant of F# minor).

These general features of Elfman's style will be seen in abundance as the *Batman* score is examined in more detail.

Unity within the score: The Bat-theme

Danny Elfman's score only has one principal theme, and it is based on the following figure:

Outline of the Bat-theme

(D major chord)

The Bat-theme is given above with no rhythmic character because Elfman uses many different rhythms to articulate it (though in practice, the distinctive minor 6th on the fourth note is often the longest note in a statement of the Bat-theme). Moreover, although presented here in C minor (which is the key in which it is most heard), it initially appears in the opening titles in B minor.

Note that the DVD of the film, in common with British television broadcasts of it, plays at 25 frames-per-second, rather than the standard 24 frames-per-second of the original 35mm film. This has the effect of playing 4% faster and thus all sound is higher in pitch than actually recorded, by just under a semitone. Thus the B minor of the opening will sound like a flat C minor. Although this phenomenon is confusing, the CD plays at the proper pitch of the score and so provides a useful reference. All references to keys, pitch and tempo are converted to conform to their original pitch, as heard on the original score recording.

It is essentially a five-note theme, with a shorter, four-note version outlined as *x* in the example above. The sixth note given in brackets is also often heard, and used as the third of a new chord (here it is D major) that suggests modulation to a new key. In fact, as discussed above with the *Spider-Man* chord progression on page 14, Elfman rarely uses these suggestions of new keys conventionally in *Batman*. Despite the D major chord suggesting a modulation to the dominant (G minor), the music normally merely carries on in its original key. Where the music does change key (with a new statement of the Bat-theme for example), it does so following the melodic contours of the music: rather like juxtaposing two keys as opposed to modulating smoothly between them.

A brief discussion of the use of the Bat-theme in the opening titles will help show some of the techniques used to develop it elsewhere.

The opening titles

The Bat-theme dominates the start of the film, under the opening titles sequence. It begins with a slow introduction in B minor, which layers the five-note theme upon itself in different rhythms. A sense of pulse and metre is elusive during this section, until the music builds to a loud, triumphant-sounding C♯ major chord, as the sixth (bracketed) note of the theme is heard for the first time. After this the music picks up into a much faster tempo: a galloping march of around 146 beats-per-minute which states the Bat-theme in a number of variants and passing through a number of different keys. This march starts in the original B minor, so here the modulation suggested by the C♯ major chord is denied. There is a good reason for this supposedly unrelated chord appearing at this point: the film title 'BATMAN' appears on the screen at precisely this point.

The fast section states the five-note theme in B minor:

First statement of Bat-theme in march section of opening titles

A second, six-note figure with a 'modulating tail' is then deployed by slightly altering the intervals after the first three notes. This pulls the music into A minor:

Batman

Variant on the Bat-theme with second modulating tail
(as heard in opening titles — The Batman Theme)

Another variant on the Bat-theme from the opening titles music seems to conflate ideas from page 14 and page 15 (the outline of the Bat-theme, and the first statement of the Bat-theme). Here the music shifts down a semitone, using a modified form of the first statement on page 15 (going to the 5th rather than minor 6th in the fourth note), then extending the original Bat-theme tail by using a descending arpeggio. Here the music pulls itself from G minor into F♯ minor:

Extended variant on the Bat-theme
(as heard in opening titles — The Batman Theme)

The fact that Elfman creates a short theme, which can also be used to 'modulate' to unrelated keys, means that the Bat-theme is flexible and organic. It has various rhythmic permutations, can be altered slightly while still being recognisable and the fact that it can suggest different keys makes it a useful tool for creating sequences from the same material. The Bat-theme therefore functions like a leitmotif in the Wagnerian sense: a short phrase, which through both melodic and rhythmic manipulation can be used to suit a number of situations while still being recognisably attached to the character of Batman.

Another cue which illustrates this very well, and in some ways appears to be modelled on the opening titles music just discussed, is 'Charge of the Batmobile'. The cue accompanies the scene where Batman sends the Batmobile into Axis Chemicals to drop a bomb and blow it up. The cue has a three-part structure which may be summarised as follows:

This music, which is actually two cues that segue in the movie ('Batsuit/Charge of the Batmobile') may be found on the movie score CD as track 15. It has been slightly edited to reduce the musical silence occupied by the bomb explosions during the scene. The timings in the chart refer to the CD, not the scene in the film.

Section	Timing	Chord Progression	Action	Music
A	0'00" – 0'24"	Cmin – Dmaj	Batman dons the Batsuit in preparation to go to Axis Chemicals; establishing shot of Axis Chemicals exterior	Slow, rhythmically indistinct introduction based on Bat-theme
B	0'24" – 1'00"	Cmin – Gmin	The Batmobile enters Axis Chemicals and deposits a bomb inside	Fast section based on Bat-theme, modulating through several keys
C	1'01" – end	Cmin – A♭	The Batmobile retreats amidst the exploding factory to the waiting Batman outside	Music based on a new idea from an earlier cue

A skeleton score of section B of the music is given below. It shows how the Bat-theme is used to modulate through several keys.

Batman

Excerpt from 'Charge of the Batmobile', showing use of Bat-theme to modulate

Although the overriding presence of the Bat-theme might lead one to suspect that Elfman's score is monothematic, this is hardly the case. If the score were truly saturated with the one theme, the listener would soon tire of hearing it and it would lose its effect. Another sub-theme which is used in Batman's scenes is the one referred to in section C of the cue 'Charge of the Batmobile'. The loud hammering out of this theme is given in skeleton form below:

Excerpt from 'Charge of the Batmobile'

As the table states, it derives from an earlier cue in the film, namely 'Descent into Mystery'. It is heard near the end of the cue:

Excerpt from 'Descent into Mystery'

This is again based on a short leitmotif idea of only three notes, which is repeated and developed within each cue. Although the theme seems exclusively to be used in connection with Batman, it is treated in two different ways here (though the Batmobile is coincidentally involved in both scenes).

> This section of the cue occurs at 1'11" into track 10 of the original score CD. The equivalent scene in the film may be found at 1h 9'25" into the DVD.

In 'Descent into Mystery', Vicki has been rescued by Batman and is taken to the Batcave out of harm's way, where he also asks her to take his research into the Joker's poison code to the press. At the stage in the cue that the above theme is heard, Vicki is shocked that the Batmobile seems to be about to collide into a rock wall, but soon realises that the Batmobile has entered the Batcave. The music seems to give the impression of being terrifying, as if in sympathy with Vicki Vale. In 'Charge of the Batmobile', however, the music occurs again at the end of the cue, though with an amplified orchestration (partly to overcome the loud sound effects) and the mood of the music is more triumphant, as the factory making Smilex is now being destroyed.

In both of these cues, Batman is in control of the situation and is imposing his will on others (Vicki Vale in the first case, the Joker and Axis in the second – though the Joker in fact escapes harm). The sub-theme might therefore be seen to represent Batman's power. It has a quite different musical quality to the Bat-theme and is therefore an effective contrast to it.

The Joker's music

The Joker, as opposed to Jack Napier (whose music tends to favour low percussive sounds and whole-tone music), has a unique relationship with music that accompanies him on screen. Firstly, unlike Batman, the Joker has no specific theme of his own, but rather appropriates a collection of musical objects, with which he seems to interact almost like a cartoon character. These objects include

Batman

a Viennese waltz in the style of Johann Strauss, the tune of *Beautiful Dreamer* by Stephen Foster (in some scenes given a kitsch Mantovani-like treatment with too much reverb and a lush close-harmony string arrangement) and songs taken from Prince's soundtrack album which are used within the film. Of these, only the waltz is composed by Elfman (in a consciously pastiche style):

The Joker's waltz theme

Secondly, the Joker reacts to the music accompanying him, either through exaggerated movements or by actually dancing to it. This is to suggest that he is aware of exactly what music is being used and is able to respond to it. This seems to be the case not just in the songs 'Partyman' and 'Trust' from the Prince album, where the music appears to be coming diegetically from the screen (but is heard far

Cartoon music, in the classic Scott Bradley/Carl Stalling mould, rarely seems far away from Elfman's music. In *Batman*, numerous short cues (such as the underscore to the newspaper headline about the cosmetics scare), with his trademark 'cascading' strings figure, introduce scenes and punctuate gestures.

louder and more consistently than could actually be the case). The Joker also seems to move and dance along with the appearances of his Viennese waltz, and happily dances along to the music of his own commercial when broadcasting about his Smilex tampering.

This play on the diegetic and non-diegetic functions of music within the film is unusual and is a way that makes the Joker's character musically very distinct from Batman's. The Joker 'steals' and appears to control a number of different kinds of music, each with their own cultural coding, while Batman, by oblivious contrast, is underscored by the late-romantic idiom of classical film scoring, all based around his own six-note theme. It is further accentuated by the fact that the Joker's music is predominantly major and Batman's predominantly minor: a strange reversal of superhero convention that nevertheless highlights the apparent exuberance and dark brooding of each character respectively.

Elfman's score and Prince's soundtrack album

The Prince album mentioned above (the motion picture *Soundtrack* album) was released as part of the film's marketing strategy before the film went on general release and the main single release 'Batdance' (which, like other tracks on the album, contains dialogue from the movie) was designed to generate both revenue and interest prior to the film reaching the screens. Furthermore, the songs on the album are written in such a way as to provide a loose narrative structure that reflects that of the film. The songs (although all performed by Prince) are explicitly written as being sung by characters from within the film (Batman, Bruce Wayne, Vicki Vale, the Joker and so on).

Although many of the songs used in the film are just short excerpts used low in the background over some scenes (such as 'The Future' at the beginning of the film or 'Electric Chair' during Bruce Wayne's charity fundraiser), two of the songs heard in a much fuller version, as mentioned above, are 'Partyman' and 'Trust', both of which are used to underscore scenes with the Joker. These both work well with the scenes in which they are used, as they uphold the portrayal of the Joker as an extrovert and carefree character, in keeping with the use of the lighter and more frivolous orchestration, waltz theme and metre given to the Joker by Elfman. However, each song hides an ironic twist: in the narrative, the Joker always has darker intentions beneath the surface (in the case of 'Partyman', the Joker is ruining countless priceless works of art to the music; in the case of 'Trust', the Joker betrays the trust of the citizens of Gotham by attempting to poison them with Smilex gas).

These songs are more than merely a commercial tie-in with the film: their use is consistent with the Joker's appropriation of musical objects and the use of popular, contemporary music by the Joker in two of his scenes contrasts sharply with the dark, orchestral underscore used for Batman.

3
Case study one

'Shootout'/'First Confrontation' (Axis Chemicals)

'Shootout' (named 'First Confrontation' on the score CD) comes at a crucial point in the first part of the film. It occurs during the police raid on Axis Chemicals, where Jack Napier and his gang of thugs have been trying to find company records. Commissioner Gordon, having learned that Eckhardt has taken on the operation himself, goes in person to take control. Meanwhile, Batman also intervenes and faces Jack Napier for the first and only time before he becomes the Joker. In the fracas, one of Napier's bullets ricochets off Batman's armour and pierces him through both cheeks. He topples backwards and although Batman tries to save him, ultimately Napier falls to his doom into a vat of acid. The police attempt to arrest Batman, but he escapes before he can be apprehended. The cue ends with the Joker's bleached white hand rising from the murky waters of the waste outlet outside the factory.

At around 5'30", this is the longest single musical cue in the whole of Elfman's score and it is tautly structured both thematically and tonally. It is divided into four main sections, matching four distinct points in the drama. The table below summarises these sections, the main keys explored by each and the relative timings of each part.

The timings are given from the original score CD and from the DVD release of the film. It will be noted that the CD version of this cue (named 'First Confrontation' as track 3) has been edited and thus does not contain all of the music from the film (some of the ostinato sections go on much longer than would be desirable in a purely-for-listening track, for example).

Section	Timing	Tonality	Action
A	0'0" (CD) / 23'49" (DVD)	Cm – B♭m – G♯m – F♯m – Cm	Napier and thugs battle with police
B	1'05" (CD) / 25'05" (DVD)	Cm – E♭m – C♯m – Bm – Cm	Batman arrives and tussles with thugs
C	1'58" (CD) / 26'16" (DVD)	Fm – whole-tone episode – B♭ – dim 7th	Batman pounces on Napier, Gordon threatened, Napier shoots Eckhardt, Napier accidentally shot by own bullet and falls into acid
D	3'55" (CD) / 28'27" (DVD)	C♯m – Cm – (Fm) – D	Batman escapes as Joker's hand emerges out of acid

As the above table shows, the cue moves through a number of keys, many unrelated to the staring point of C minor. In addition, the end of the cue is in a new key (D) and this is significant for three reasons. Firstly, the new key is major and this alone provides a sense of conclusion to the cue (like a sort of tierce de Picardie but in the 'wrong key'). Secondly, it is the key that announces the Joker's 'birth' within the narrative. This is significant because D is the key of his waltz and furthermore makes the link with the Joker and major keys: previously Jack Napier had principally been associated with the whole-tone scale. Thirdly, the progressive tonality of this cue mirrors that implied by the Bat-theme itself, namely that it starts in C minor and ends on a D major chord.

Thematic layers within the cue

'Shootout' is based principally on a rocking ostinato first heard in cellos and double basses, soon to be joined by viola (first three notes) and low piano:

Opening bass ostinato

It will be noticed that a certain instability is suggested by the music rocking between C and F♯ (a tritone). As extra layers are added during the cue, A♮ is sounded above this too to form all of the notes of a diminished 7th – a chord full of tension and traditionally associated with suspense. It will also be noticed that the above ostinato sounds unmistakably as if it should be in ⁶⁄₈, but the cue is notated in ³⁄₄ throughout. One reason for this is that, as with much of Elfman's music, the music is comprised of many rhythmic layers, containing a number of cross-rhythms. Some of these layers are best 'heard' in ³⁄₄. Moreover, the several statements of the Bat-theme that occur during the cue are all in ³⁄₄.

One wonders whether ³⁄₄ was chosen for convenience within *Performer*, too. ⁶⁄₈ has traditionally had its problems with sequencing software, as tempo is normally set by crotchets in compound time rather than the expected dotted crotchet.

Much of the bustle of this cue is created by the insistent opening ostinato and the building up of rhythmic fragments around it. Elfman seems to stick to a set number of rhythmic ideas and to vary the melodic content of them in subsequent statements. When the key of the music changes, all fragments are often restated in the new key. Here are three pairs of rhythmic ideas (some suggesting ⁶⁄₈, some suggesting ³⁄₄) that illustrate this:

Batman

Ostinato layer one

Prevailing key: Cm

Prevailing key: Cm

Ostinato layer two

Prevailing key: C#m

Prevailing key: C#m

Ostinato layer three

Prevailing key: Cm

Prevailing key: E♭m

However, there are also examples of even more intricate cross-rhythm. In the following example, a trumpet figure cuts across both $\frac{3}{4}$ and $\frac{6}{8}$, suggesting $\frac{3}{16}$ or a division of the bar into four beats:

Muted trumpet cross-rhythm

It should be pointed out that a number of the rhythmic fragments used in this cue above the bass line are based on either repeated notes or the interval of a semitone. These work well above the ostinato bass and maintain both tension and momentum. In addition, the fact that each of these fragments rarely lasts more than a bar means that they can be passed around the orchestra rapidly, creating a constantly evolving patchwork of rhythmic activity and timbre.

Use of the whole-tone scale

The whole-tone scale is listed above as one of Elfman's favourite compositional gambits, and has furthermore been allied to the character of Jack Napier in discussing the present cue. The whole-tone scale in music has special significance here, as it traditionally represents stasis (because all of the intervals within the scale are equal) or instability (because the tritone can be formed from within the scale).

The whole-tone scale on C

Elfman uses the whole-tone scale during section C in the above table, where the tension in the scene is at its apex. Here it is uncertain what will happen as Commissioner Gordon is threatened and Batman and Napier are struggling, so the whole-tone scale seems appropriate. There is a reliance in this section on sparse textures (sustained pads, piano chords, high string effects), which is in sharp contrast to the busy music (and emphasis on brass, strings and percussion) that has been heard previously. This in its own way adds to the tension and focuses attention on the dialogue and acting of the protagonists.

Tonality in 'Shootout'

Keys play an important part in the organisation and scoring of 'Shootout'. Its progressive tonality has already been mentioned, though it is clear that C minor is the principal key throughout. It is the key in which Batman's theme is heard the first and last times within the cue (it also occurs in E♭ minor and C♯ minor) and seems to be a reference point for sections of this scene involving Batman and the police. The fact that both the police and Batman seem to work mostly within this key underlines their will to bring Napier's gang to justice.

Countering this is the destructive force of Napier and his henchmen. In sections A and B, where Jack Napier is destroying chemical equipment or playing with controls to thwart the police, the tonality shifts downwards in sequence twice by a tone. In other words, as Napier first interferes with the controls of the machine controlling large vats of chemicals in section A, the music moves from B♭ minor to G♯ minor to F♯ minor in sequence. This has the effect of moving the music away from the 'safe haven' of C minor. Only when the scene cuts away from Napier do we return to C minor and see Batman enter the fray. A similar process happens in section B, where Napier punches a hole in a vat of chemicals with an axe. The music (previously in E♭ minor) is driven through Napier's sequence into C♯ minor, then B minor, before being restored to C minor by the next shot of Batman, as he punches one of Napier's approaching henchmen in the face. In both of these examples, we can see that Napier's scenes drive the music's key *down* along the whole-tone scale, whereas Batman's changes of key (F♯ minor to C minor, C minor to E♭ minor) either restore the tonality back *up* to C minor or drive it on to a higher key.

As the scene works into section C, the music ramps up to F minor from Batman's C minor, as Napier looks for an escape route. As the subdominant of C minor, this is one of the few conventional harmonic progressions within the cue and serves to heighten the tension at this crucial point. The multi-layered ostinati now give way to a more uniform repeated-chord figure in strings, though still with a cross-rhythm present in the bass:

Bass cross-rhythm

As Napier realises he might have a chance of shooting Commissioner Gordon, the music suddenly calms and enters the whole-tone section mentioned above. Despite Batman's intervention, no Bat-theme is stated during this whole section and no firm tonality is established, save for a suggestion of D major as Bob shouts out 'Let's go!' to Napier. This is telling, as it is the Joker's key, suggesting that at this point Napier might win the battle. However, this is not to be. After Napier's own bullet sends him toppling over the rail and Batman tries to rescue him, the music ends on a sustained B♭, which then clashes with an E major chord (note the tritonal harmonic progression) and acts as an appoggiatura against it. A series of diminished 7th chords and general orchestral cacophony accompany Napier's fall and the music then flows through B♭ and alights on C♯ minor, as Batman tries to regain control of the situation and make his escape. After being dominated by whole-tone music, a statement of the Bat-theme in C♯ minor accompanies his escape. The music shifts to its 'home' key of C minor once more when we see Batman outside the factory, thus suggesting that he has escaped safely. A cut to the waste outlets shows that Napier has survived as the music concludes on D major:

End scene music — Joker survives

Keen-eared listeners may notice on the CD track that there is a premonition of the Joker's waltz in this cue after Batman has dropped Napier in the acid. It occurs in C♯ minor, 4'05" into the track. In the movie however, this is all but inaudible, with the sound effects of Batman making his escape being far louder at that point.

Conclusion

The above discussion should go some way towards elucidating the principal elements of 'Shootout'. The cue has a tight structure which changes according to the action on-screen (every change of key hits something important within the drama or hits a specific cut). Tonality also helps to place Batman and Napier within the narrative, while the orchestral writing bears many of the hallmarks of a classic Elfman score: layered ostinati, use of the whole-tone scale, cross-rhythms and prominent use of the tritone.

4
Case study two

'Challenge/Dream'/'Childhood Remembered'

'Challenge/Dream' (named 'Childhood Remembered' on the score CD) happens just before the last act of the drama unfolds. Bruce Wayne remembers when his parents were murdered and realises that it was the Joker, in his past life as Jack Napier, who was responsible for the crime. It is a pivotal point which spurs Batman into action against the Joker in the final part of the movie. The majority of the cue is played as a flashback, which calls for a very different treatment both in Burton's direction and in Elfman's score.

> This scene occurs at 1h 25'47" into the DVD.

The sound of 'Challenge/Dream'

Just as one of the stock-in-trade devices of flashbacks in film is the use of slow-motion, so is the use of a lot of reverb in film and television music. This is one of the devices used by Elfman and his mix engineers on this cue. The addition of a great deal of reverb makes the music sound more distant, intangible and less clear-cut, just as a memory is never as precise in recollection as the events being remembered.

The music, which is in A minor throughout, has an atmospheric, spooky and tragic tone, helped by the delicate scoring: Elfman uses synthesiser tracks, voices (particularly female voices), strings and a solo violin. Against this, there is a persistent, ominous bass drum thud which punctuates the music and a very low and rhythmic piano part, coupled initially with snare drum. It is important to note that this piano part is not treated with extra reverb; it remains crisp and menacing all the way through the cue. Moreover, it is undoubtedly an instrument that Elfman has intended to represent Jack Napier (or at least his threat) within this cue. It is a timbre which has been associated with Napier in some of the earliest cues of the film, such as the scene where he pays Eckhardt ('Jack vs Eckhart' [sic] or 'Shootout').

The presence of the piano throughout this cue is crucial in maintaining pace and giving the music rhythmic impetus. It resurfaces occasionally to remind the viewer that this is not a pleasant flashback, though it stops altogether after the point when Bruce's parents are shot. Although octave leaps are used (down to the bottom A of the piano), only A is sounded by the piano part, hammering out the tonic of the key, even when the harmony seems to move away from it. This can be seen in the skeleton score of the example below. This example occurs shortly into the cue after the cello ostinato has been established, and implies a move to

C major as Bruce examines the dossier on his parents' death, before returning to A minor:

Excerpt from 'Challenge/Dream'

This excerpt occurs at 0'22" on the CD track 'Childhood Remembered'. The CD track follows the music of the film faithfully, with only a short edit in the middle of the cue, where the silence in the film after the shooting is shortened.

Use of collage technique

Although Elfman keeps a sense of pulse by reiterating a figure in the piano (marked *z* in the example above), once the cue plunges into flashback this is not regularly deployed and is interchanged with single quaver notes on the low A. The regularity set up by the start of the cue, including the tonal stability and use of ostinati, is broken down once the film enters Bruce's memories. The change is signalled by the cello ostinato fading out and a prominent synth pitch-bend down (this occurs around 1h 26'30" into the DVD). Elfman here alters the texture of the music: most of the 'secure' bass line (synth pad and low strings) is dropped in favour of floating, higher textures, thus removing any sense of grounded tonality. The only element which remains is the menacing piano and at this point Elfman adds a booming bass drum, which seems to add a fateful sense of ominousness to the cue.

Once the music enters the flashback, the vocal sounds (these sound synthesised, but may be heavily processed real vocals) enter and the music is built up of constantly shifting collage-like textures, with the pitch-bend (always down) feature being prominent among the synth lines. The music is made up of rhythmically indistinct layers, often suggesting other keys away from A minor. Because tonal and rhythmic regularity has been removed from the music, it takes on a ghostly, amorphous character which sounds unstable and creepy. Moreover, in addition to the pitch-bend feature mentioned above, several parts have a kind of 'sighing' figure of a falling semitone from F to E (sometimes starting from E itself):

Sighing motif used in Challenge/Dream

The solo violin part in this cue, which might be seen to represent the young Bruce himself, lost and alone in his memories, occasionally uses glissando to match the pitch-bend of the synthesised textures.

In the context of the key of A minor, F and E are the minor 6th and 5th of the scale respectively. This could be seen as a reference to the Bat-theme (the fourth and fifth notes), which is otherwise unstated. More immediately, it is a figure which is traditionally associated with sorrow or despair – very appropriate for the scene.

Once Bruce's parents have been shot, Jack Napier steps out of the shadows and here the low strings of the orchestra have an upwards glissando gesture, which neatly answers the downward pitch-bending heard previously. It is also a reference to a larger gesture heard as the Joker steps out of the shadows in Grissom's apartment shortly after surgery.

This earlier glissando gesture may be heard on the DVD at 36'12". It is not featured on the score CD.

Tonality from 'Challenge/Dream' to 'Batsuit/Charge of the Batmobile'

Although 'Challenge/Dream' is essentially an extended tonic pedal of A minor (albeit with some suggestions of other keys and chords), it has an interesting relationship with the tonality of the next two scenes and of the film in general. In the majority of cues involving Batman, flat minor keys are used (C minor, D minor, Eb minor and so on). Bruce Wayne's music, insofar as it derives from the Bat-theme, seems to be of a simpler, even blander kind, both tonally and in terms of orchestration. In 'Challenge/Dream', this seems to be borne out through the cello ostinato and use of A minor itself, the simplest minor key with no sharps or flats in its key signature. There may also be a link to childhood innocence and simplicity (especially with suggestions of C major) that is appropriate to Bruce reliving his childhood memories.

The most important aspect of the cue tonally is that it prepares for the resolution to C major of a theme heard earlier which is based on the Bat-theme. As Bruce leaves his flashback, he turns to find that Alfred has let Vicki into the Bat-cave. The ensuing discussion is a resolution between them of the anxieties and tension behind Bruce's secrecy. Importantly, this following cue (called 'Tender Batcave' in the score and appearing as 'Love Theme' on the CD) moves from G major to C major. The love theme itself is based on the Bat-theme. It is heard at the beginning of this cue in G major:

Love theme in G major

The theme is only different to the Bat-theme by virtue of having the second note flattened and then being re-harmonised, making it a very economical theme. It is associated with Bruce Wayne and scenes involving Vicki, but the link with the Bat-theme also suggests Batman, who, in a sense, is the barrier between them.

The cue 'Bruce Contemplates/ Photos' (given on the CD as 'Photos/Beautiful Dreamer') shows neatly how both Bruce and the Joker objectify Vicki as a romantic target, and the differing musical means used. It also highlights the differences in orchestration between the bland Bruce Wayne and the outlandish Joker. The scene occurs at 49'47" on the DVD.

'Tender Batcave' moves the music tonally to the 'correct' key for Batman's resolution (C major), though the love theme is not stated at the end of the cue. This is because, despite Bruce and Vicki having made peace with each other, the Joker is still at large and Bruce has to 'go to work'. This ushers in the C minor territory of Batman once more as Bruce dons the Batsuit and sends the Batmobile in to destroy Axis Chemicals.

The love theme itself is not heard in C major properly until the very end of the film, where it doubles as a metamorphosis of the Bat-theme. It is heard in blazing full orchestra in the finale:

Final statement of love-theme/altered Bat-theme in C major

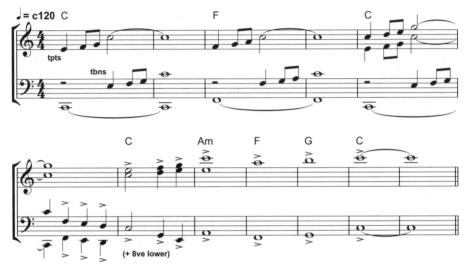

This makes sense, in that the brooding Batman, whose music starts rhythmically and is tonally unstable in the opening titles of the film, latches on to C minor as a 'home key' and then, when all is resolved for his character, converts this into an affirmative C major with a triumphant march rhythm. The chromatic tail of the theme (which tended to pull the music away from its centre) is removed, with the Bat-theme and the love theme becoming one.

> The last few bars of this excerpt have led some commentators to compare the ending with the end of the famous introduction to Strauss's *Also sprach Zarathustra*, which shares its key.

Conclusion

'Challenge/Dream' is an important cue in the context of Elfman's score, as it is a reflective moment that contrasts with the heavy, ostinato-led action sequences and outlandish orchestrations of the Joker's music. It is a cue which makes more use of synthetic and sound-design textures and effective mix engineering than most of the rest of the score. The intimate and delicate scoring paves the way for the next cue, which takes the unresolved D minor chord at the conclusion of 'Dream', and moves through G major to a temporary resolution of C major. It is no accident that this C major is the relative of A minor and the tonal relationship between these cues (from 'Challenge/Dream' to 'Batsuit/Charge of the Batmobile') shows that Elfman has an acute tonal awareness and is able to deploy keys conventionally in his writing from one cue to the next.

5
Case study three

'Waltz (to the Death)'

Towards the end of the movie, before the Joker plunges to his death from the top of Gotham cathedral, there is a prolonged chase sequence up the cathedral. Once Batman reaches the top, he has to deal with a number of henchmen while the Joker dances with Vicki Vale to an imaginary waltz. This waltz is heard non-diegetically as an extended reprise of the Joker's waltz from earlier, but the editing of the film and the Joker's dancing are such that once again the music seems to be controlled by the Joker. Moreover, Batman's struggles are so well-timed with the music that it seems that the Joker is trying to control him within his waltz, like a kind of grim choreography that Batman is forced to follow.

This cue, simply called 'Waltz' in the score, but labelled 'Waltz to the Death' as track 18 on the score CD, involves an introduction as the first goon is dealt with, which is not really part of the main waltz. The waltz referred to in the table below starts after this first conflict. The whole scene starts at 1h 46'10" into the DVD, after the Joker's line: 'Shall we dance?'.

Structure of the waltz

The waltz is a rigorously organised rondo (AABACADAE), as the table below elucidates. Also indicated are the relative tempi of sections in beats per minute (bpm) and their relative length in bars.

Section	Key	Length (bars)	Tempo (bpm)
Intro	D	4	c.186
A	D	15	c.180–186
A	D	16	c.180-186
B	D–A–B♭	26	c.180–186
A	E♭	16	c.180–186
C	D min	16	c.180–186
A	E♭	34	c.195–204
D	E	13	c.200
A	E	19	c.192
C	E min	16	c.186

Batman

Section	Key	Length (bars)	Tempo (bpm)
A	E	12	c.186
E (interruption)	B	N/A (waltz fades out)	N/A (waltz fades out)

The table makes some important facts clear immediately. Firstly, this is a waltz which, during Batman's struggles, seems to intensify by getting faster and higher in pitch. Secondly, the Joker's own sections of the scene, where he talks to the unresponsive Vicki, are tonally stable (normally A and C sections), whereas Batman's sections (mainly B and D, as well as statements of A) go through a number of keys before alighting on the key of the new A section.

By stating the Joker's waltz theme in progressively higher keys (D, then Eb, then E), Elfman makes the sections of the music follow the tension of the scene. It is important that the B and D sections above, which feature Batman's struggles, tend to move chromatically through keys and to suggest a number of different keys within each section before modulating to the key of the new A section. Thus the tonal struggle within the music in sections B and D mirrors the physical struggles Batman has to face on screen. A closer examination of the B section of the waltz will help clarify this:

B section of the waltz

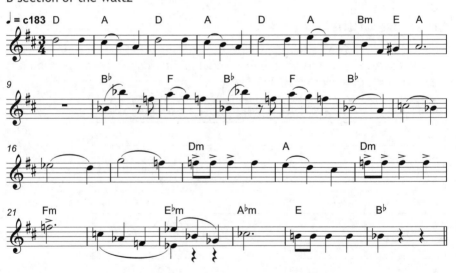

Here it can be seen how, despite starting fairly predictably with a modulation to the dominant bars 7–8 of the extract, the music then moves rapidly from one key to another, accelerating towards the end of the section as it gets more remote from the starting point of D major. Furthermore, Elfman's cadence at the end of the section uses a tritonal progression (E to B♭) as an unconventional preparation for the new key of E♭.

The Joker's sections of the waltz also seem to reflect his mock persona on screen. The two occurrences of the melancholic C section (once in D minor, once in E minor), for example, are more sedate and delicately scored, allowing for the Joker's dialogue to be heard clearly (it is conversely no surprise that when Batman is on screen, the brass section is amplified in the orchestration to compensate for the sound effects of his fights). The Joker feints a melancholic air as the music responds to him:

First C section in D minor, excerpt

Of course, he does this only to unleash a gag on the hapless Vicki, but it is interesting that the Joker, who has so far mainly been associated with major-key music, is using minor-key music here in order to show his sensitive side. Ironically, all the while this is happening, Batman is being 'made to dance' to predominantly major-key music, when he has previously been associated with dark minor keys.

The effect of the waltz, with its overblown garish orchestration (sounding at its fastest more like a demonic circus-ride steam-organ than a sophisticated Viennese waltz) is to give the whole scene a bittersweet character. Although Batman is in danger and is effectively being worn down by the Joker's henchmen, the regular pulse and colourful decorations of the music lend it a dark humour. Only when he has defeated the last of the Joker's henchmen in the belfry is Batman able to apply himself wholly to defeating the Joker. The waltz fades rapidly as an unhindered Batman is spied by Vicki. She contrives to distract the Joker while Batman prepares to attack him. All of this happens over an unresolved pedal outlining the dominant of E, the chord upon which the waltz is interrupted, since Batman denies the Joker's stable E major tonality by interrupting the flow of the waltz through attacking him. The music shifts around the B, adding the seventh A and other notes which seem to weaken the tonal feel of the music hitherto. All of a sudden, the Joker's position seems precarious, and the strength afforded him by his waltz music vanishes with it. The last statement of the A section in E major is denied the tonic, which is a neat tonal equivalent for the interruption that Batman is about to make.

Conclusion

The waltz towards the end of the film is the Joker's last real position of power within the narrative. It articulates the attempts of his various henchmen to thwart Batman and has a key structure which helps underpin both the sections of dialogue and Batman's struggles in trying to rescue Vicki. The waltz shows also the very strong 'set-piece' structure of Elfman's score: despite having a number of recurring themes for unity, many of the cues have their own discrete structure and style that makes them effective as 'stand-alone' pieces. Moreover, it is interesting that the two statements of the Joker's waltz seem to frame his involvement in the movie: the first as he shoots Grissom and his power is in the ascendancy; the second at the film's dénouement, where his power is about to be snuffed out.

6
Legacy and influence

The vitality and breadth of Elfman's compositional technique seems to reach maturity in the *Batman* score and it is no surprise that, having shown what he could do with a large budget and a potential summer blockbuster, Elfman has been in great demand as a composer ever since. The score itself became the basis for Elfman's second *Batman* film, in which the dark and gothic tone of the original is more accentuated. It seems that the score for *Batman Returns* owes almost as much in this respect to Elfman's score for *Edward Scissorhands*, which many critics regard as his masterpiece.

Elfman did not return to score the third *Batman* film (*Batman Forever*), following Tim Burton's own decision not to direct it. Elliot Goldenthal's music for this 1995 film seems to try to break away from Elfman's own distinctive theme, but still retains its dark minor/major character. The music for the animated *Batman* series similarly owes to Elfman's 1989 score.

Interestingly, the subsequent *Batman* films (*Batman and Robin* 1997) shrugged off much of the sinister style of the previous Burton films and leaned more towards asking the camp humour of the 1960s television series. Elliot Goldenthal's music retains the same theme that was used for the caped crusader's previous outing, but matches more closely the lighter tone of the film.

The most recent Batman film (*Batman Begins* 2005) seems to have brought the genre around full circle. Acting as a form of prequel to the 1989 film, but updating the style and characters, this is another dark rendering of the Batman legend. The score, by Hans Zimmer and James Newton Howard, is a little more neutral than any of the previous *Batman* series. Although it is a more darkly toned score than either of the Goldenthal offerings, it lacks the distinctive character of either those or the Elfman series.

Because of Batman's mysterious nature and the accentuation of this within Burton's and Elfman's interpretation of the Batman legend, Elfman's treatment of the superhero in scoring terms (as opposed to the style of John Williams' *Superman* theme of 1978, for example) was radically different. Since *Batman*, there has been a tendency for superhero themes to have an ambivalent edge to them, perhaps using minor keys in an awe-inspiring context rather than a melancholic or tragic one (Elfman's own score to *Spider-Man* is an excellent example of this). It is no accident that Elfman was asked to score several similar comic-book transfers after *Batman*; scores like *Dick Tracy*, *Spider-Man* and *Spider-Man 2*, and *Hulk* seem to bear this tendency out. Despite this, Elfman has been keen not to be typecast within the genres of films he has scored (hence projects such as *Black Beauty*, *Men in Black* and the rearranging of Herrmann's *Psycho* for Gus van Sant's remake).

As has been mentioned before, Elfman's style was at its most emulated during the early to mid-1990s and has evolved over the last few years to encompass a wider range of scoring techniques. However, it is fair to say that the essence of his musical language has remained unchanged, and it is this language which is shown very clearly in the music written for *Batman*.

The *Psycho* score, while being part of a dubious experiment to recreate Hitchcock's classic film shot-for-shot, was clearly a labour of love for Elfman. He has often cited Herrmann as one his major influences and models, partly through a love of watching many of the films he scored as a movie-going child and teenager.

7
Glossary

Accidental. A symbol in front of a note that indicates a change of pitch from the expected note. Accidentals include the sharp (♯) to indicate raising the note by a semitone and the flat (♭) to indicate lowering it by a semitone. The natural (♮) indicates that the note should be neither sharpened nor flattened.

Amplified. Put through an amplifier (amp). Informally, the term is often used to mean making a sound louder, but this is not necessarily always the case.

Analogue. Refers to a signal that directly represents variable data (such as sound or video images), as opposed to **digital** in which such signals are represented by a stream of numbers. Analogue recording media (such as records or cassettes) store the sound using a continuously varying signal.

Appoggiatura. A momentary dissonance occurring on the beat, which usually resolves upwards or downwards by step. Sometimes referred to as a 'leaning note' for this reason.

Audio. Sound or hearing. Often used in the expression 'audio signal', referring to an electrical signal that uses variations (for example in voltage) to convey information that can be converted to sound by a loudspeaker.

Balance. The relative volume levels between instruments.

bpm. Beats per minute. Refers to the tempo of a piece. If there are 60 beats-per-minute (60 bpm) there will be one beat-per-second. 120 bpm is twice as fast – one beat every half-second.

Canon. A musical device (sometimes an entire piece) in which a melody in one part fits with the same melody in another part even though the latter starts a few beats later. The device occurs in the type of song known as a round.

CD. Compact disc. A popular **digital** recording format. It first appeared in 1982 and by 1988 sales of CDs were already surpassing sales of vinyl records.

Chord. A combination of notes played at the same time to create harmony. Often denoted by symbols, eg Cm, F♯^{7}.

Chorus.
1 A section of a song which returns several times.
2 A group of singers.
3 An electronic effect used to thicken a sound by combining slightly altered versions of sound with the original signal.
4 MIDI controller 93, which is used to adjust the chorus (thickening) level applied to a sound.

Conductor. Musician responsible for shaping an ensemble's performance, including matters of tempo, cohesion, tone, dynamics and interpretation. In film sessions, the role of keeping players in time is largely negated by the use of a click track, but the conductor is essential for the smooth running of the recording session, answering queries and keeping the orchestra on schedule. In practice, if no conductor is specially appointed, this role is undertaken by the orchestrator or composer.

Controller.
1 A MIDI input device such as a keyboard or electronic wind instrument.
2 A type of MIDI message, which can be used for controlling aspects of the sound such as volume or reverb.

Copyist. Someone who generates and duplicates parts for the individual players of ensemble music, often also binding and duplicating the master full score. The process is now greatly aided by computer software such as Sibelius.

Chromatic. An adjective describing notes outside the current key or mode that are added for colour (the word chromatic meaning 'coloured') and that do not cause a change of key. Accidentals are not necessarily chromatic.

Clef. A symbol defining the pitches of the notes on a stave.

Click track. An audible metronome fed through headphones to performers, in order to keep them in time. Where this is based on the tempo map of a given cue or sequence, satisfactory synchronisation of music and video can be obtained.

Contrapuntal. A contrapuntal texture uses counterpoint, which is the simultaneous use of two or more melodies with independent rhythms. There may be some imitation between the parts, but counterpoint can also be non-imitative. Whole movements may be contrapuntal, or the music may alternate between contrapuntal and other textures. The term is now often used interchangeably with polyphony.

Countermelody. A tune written to work in counterpoint with a theme, often added to provide textural variety.

Cue. A piece of music composed to fit a specific scene or section of a film.

Data. Information. Data can take different forms such as audio, video, MIDI and text.

Delay. An effect which produces a copy of the input sound signal, which lags behind the input by a specified amount. Delay is used as an effect in its own right, but it is also a component of **ADT, chorus, flange** and **phasing**.

Diatonic. Describes music that only uses the notes of the scale of the given key (in other words, it does not require unexpected accidentals).

Diegetic. Music which appears to originate from something on screen (for example a car radio, someone playing the piano, music from a hi-fi). Sometimes referred to as 'source music' or 'in-vision music'.

Digital. Refers to a signal which is encoded as numbers. When sound is digitised, the original **analogue** signal is represented by a stream of numbers, and can thus be stored in, and manipulated by, a computer system.

Drum machine. A device that offers a range of synthesised and/or sampled percussion sounds, and the means to sequence them into rhythm patterns.

Dynamics. The degree of loudness in music. This is indicated in scores by symbols such as $\boldsymbol{p}$ (*piano* = quiet), $\boldsymbol{f}$ (*forte* = loud) and ◁———— (*crescendo* = gradually increasing in volume).

Editing. The art of manipulating data (such as a computer file or recording) in order to improve it or to produce something different. Editing a recording originally involved splicing and looping bits of tape, but nowadays it is mostly done with digital processing.

Effects. A term used to describe a variety of sound processing techniques such as reverb, delay, chorus, flange and phasing. It also commonly refers to devices which carry out these tasks.

EQ. Equalisation. Any control that adjusts the relative frequency components of a sound, such as tone controls (treble, mid, bass).

Headphones. A pair of loudspeakers small enough to fit over the ears so that sounds can be heard by an individual with minimal disturbance to others in the vicinity.

Flange. A sweeping **delay** effect in which the delay-time is continuously changing. The name originates from the flange on the outside of a tape reel, which if pressed by an engineer varied the speed of the playback with respect to another, identical reel.

Key signature. A set of sharps or flats that determines which key the following music is to be played in (although **accidentals** within the course of the music may change that key).

Legato. Smooth. A musical line without gaps between notes, often shown in music notation by a curved line above or below the notes affected. The opposite of **staccato**.

Metronome. A mechanical or electronic device which produces a click or beep at a regular and adjustable rate in order to determine a tempo and regular pulse for music. A metronome mark of = 60 (or MM=60) is the same as 60bpm and means one beat per second.

Mickey-Mousing. A faintly pejorative term which refers to music that mimics the action on screen. So called because this device is a stock-in-trade of cartoon music.

MIDI. Musical Instrument Digital Interface. A standard protocol for connecting and remotely operating electronic instruments and related devices such as computers and effects units.

MIDI channel. One of 16 possible instrumental tracks of data that can be accommodated from a single **MIDI port**.

MIDI file. A computer data file which stores sequences of MIDI information.

MIDI port. A device in (or attached to) a computer which allows it to communicate with MIDI instruments.

Mixing. The art of blending together separate audio tracks. This may include adjusting their **balance, stereo panning** and **EQ**, as well as adding **effects**.

Mock-up. A sketch of a cue using synthesisers and/or samplers in place of real instruments, designed to give an idea of what the final orchestrated cue might sound like. In film music, the mock-up is often what the director will hear in order to approve the cue for orchestration.

Modulation.
1 A musical term for a change of key.
2 A technical term relating to one signal being modified by another, often when a sound is altered in pitch by another waveform.
3 A MIDI controller message type 1, which controls the amount of vibrato.

Monitor.
1 To listen to (or measure) an audio signal, either via headphones or via monitor speakers.
2 The visual display unit (VDU or screen) used in a computer or video system.

Motif. A short thematic strand of only a few notes. Music which is motivic may be considered to be made up of several of these short strands.

Muted.
1 An instruction to an instrumentalist (*con sordino* in Italian) to use a mute to muffle the sound.
2 The temporary silencing of a recorded audio track.

Non-diegetic. Music which has been composed to accompany events on screen but which is visibly not part of the action (for example music to accompany a car chase or to highlight the emotions of a conversation between two characters). Also referred to as 'underscore' or 'incidental' music.

Orchestrator. Musician who works with a composer to produce full orchestral scores of cues from 'sketches', mock-ups or short scores. The process may involve filling out harmonies, adding detail such as counter-melodies and the doubling and redistributing of parts.

Ostinato. A repeating melodic or rhythmic pattern heard throughout a substantial passage of music. In popular music and jazz a melodic ostinato is known as a **riff**.

Pedal, or 'pedal point'. A sustained or repeated note against which changing harmonies are heard. A pedal on the dominant creates excitement and the feeling that the tension must be resolved by moving to the tonic. A pedal on the tonic anchors the music to its key note. A pedal can be created, for example, on both tonic and dominant – a double pedal. If a pedal occurs in an upper part, rather than the bass, it is called an inverted pedal.

Pitch. The height or depth of a note. This can be relative and expressed as an interval (such as a tone or semitone) between two notes, or it can be an absolute quality determined by the number of vibrations per second of a string, a column of air or a membrane.

Pitch-bend.
1 A deviation in the pitch of a note, used for expressive effect in pop music and jazz.
2 The MIDI message for inflecting the pitch, up or down, of all the notes on a given MIDI channel.

Pizzicato. Plucked – a technique used by string players instead of bowing the strings.

Polyphonic. The simultaneous use of two or more notes, or melodies. The term is now used interchangeably with counterpoint.

Polyrhythm. The simultaneous combination of two or more distinctly different and often conflicting types of rhythm.

Reverb. Short for reverberation. The complex series of reflections that occurs when sound is created in an enclosed space. Often artificially added to a recording – originally by mechanical spring or plate devices, but now more commonly produced digitally.

Riff. A short repeating melodic pattern heard throughout a passage of music. A riff is a type of **ostinato**.

Rondo. A musical form which alternates between a theme or section in the home key and episodes which modulate away from it. The standard thematic plan for a rondo is ABACABA, where A, B and C are different both thematically and tonally.

Rubato. Literally 'robbed time'. Expressive changes to the position of beats within a bar, sometimes leading to expressive fluctuations in the overall tempo (common in some types of Romantic music).

Sampler. A device for recording sections of sound (samples) as digital information. It allows them to be played back with various modifications (for example at different speeds, in continuous loops or in combination with other samples).

Scale. A series of notes in ascending (or descending) order. The type of scale (for example major, minor, blues) is determined by the order of the tone and semitone gaps between the notes.

Semitone. Half a tone. The smallest commonly used interval in western tonal music (for example from E to F, or F to F♯).

Sequence.
1 Musical performance data recorded on a sequencer. Also used as a verb (to sequence) meaning to produce a sequence.
2 The *immediate* repetition at a different pitch of a phrase or motif in a continuous melodic line.

Sequencer. A device (or computer software) for the input, editing, storage and play-back of musical performance data using (at least in the last 20 years) MIDI. Sequencers may include other facilities, such as the ability to convert performance data to music notation or to combine sampled sounds with MIDI data.

SMPTE. A standard timing code (in hours, minutes, seconds and frames) used in the synchronisation of sound and music to moving pictures. The letters are an acronym for the Society of Motion Picture and Television Engineers, who invented it.

Software. A computer program – a series of instructions which determines how the hardware of a computer will respond.

Staccato. Notes that are performed shorter than printed so that each is detached from its neighbours. Often shown in notation by dots above or below the notes affected. The opposite of **legato**.

Stereo. An abbreviation of stereophonic. The use of two audio tracks to represent a solid sound image (stereo is Greek for solid), reflecting the way that humans perceive sounds through two ears.

Stereo panning. The position (left to right) of a sound in **stereo**.

Synchronisation. The process of combining music and film. Usually handled within a sequencer, sometimes communicating externally with a video recorder using timecode (SMPTE).

Syncopation. Off-beat accents or accents on weak beats.

Synthesiser. An electronic instrument that can produce and modify sound. It can be used to imitate other musical instruments and to produce non-musical sounds.

Tempo. The speed of the underlying beat in a piece of music. This may be indicated by a general description (for example fast, or allegro), be shown by a precise speed expressed in bpm, or given as a metronome mark.

Theme. A musical idea which is reused and developed throughout a composition. In film music, themes are often used to represent characters, objects or ideas from within the drama.

Tierce de Picardie. A tonic major close to a phrase or piece in the minor key.

Timbre. The quality that makes one sound (for example of a flute) different from another (for example a trumpet), even though both may be playing the same pitch at the same volume. Timbre results from complex sound waves. Even one instrument can change the timbre of a note by using by such methods as varying the attack and dynamic level, or by using different methods of note production (for example by plucking a violin instead of bowing it, or by using a mute).

Time signature. Numbers at the start of a passage of music which show the pattern of beats that make up a bar. For instance ⁴⁄₄ indicated four crotchets (or quarter-notes) per bar, while ³⁄₈ indicates three quavers (or eighth-notes) per bar. c is another way of writing ⁴⁄₄ and ¢ is the equivalent of ²⁄₂.

Tone.
1 An interval of two semitones, e.g. C–D.
2 A sound of definite pitch.
3 The timbre (quality, for example a harsh tone) of a particular instrument or voice.

Track. A part of a sequencer or recording that is used to store one or more discrete elements of the full texture, such as a drum track on a sequencer or, on two-track stereo, the data for each of the two channels (left and right).

Transpose. To move all the notes in a passage of music up or down by the same amount. This will change the key unless the transposition is by 12 semitones, which will merely change the octave.

Tritone. The interval of either a diminished 5th or an augmented 4th. Traditionally known as the *diabolus in musica* (devil in music) because of its unnatural, dissonant sound. Its use (both melodically and harmonically) is a stock-in-trade of Danny Elfman's style.

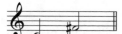 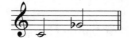

Vibrato. Small but repeating fluctuations in pitch used by performers to give warmth and expression to their tone.

Volume. The loudness of a sound, particularly in reference to the sound intensity control on an amplifier or mixer.

Waltz. A dance in triple metre (usually ³⁄₄) associated with polite society in the 19th century. Typically fairly brisk, one-in-a-bar feel (♩=60) and recognisably melodic in character with an 'oom-cha-cha' accompaniment. Significant composers of waltzes include Johann Strauss, Tchaikovsky and Chopin.

Whole-tone scale. A six-note scale made up entirely of intervals a tone away from the previous note. There are only two transpositions of the scale:

8
Bibliography and web resources

Bibliography

Brown, R. S. *Overtones and Undertones: Reading Film Music*. University of California Press, 1994

Halfyard, J. K. *Danny Elfman's Batman: A Film Score Guide*. Scarecrow Press, 2004

Halliwell, L. and Walker, J. *Halliwell's Film DVD & Video Guide 2007*. London: Harper Collins, 2006

Karlin, F. and Wright, R. *On Track: A Guide to Contemporary Film Scoring*. London: Routledge, 2004

Le Blanc, M. and Odell, C. *Tim Burton*. London: Pocket Essentials, 2001

Prendergast, R. M. *Film Music: A Neglected Art*. New York: W&W Norton, 1992

Web resources

www.imdb.com – an indispensible resource for film trivia, plotlines and filmographies

http://elfman.filmmusic.com/ – a Danny Elfman fansite, with a lot of useful background interviews and information

http://en.wikipedia.org/wiki/Batman – a handy background to the Batman legend in its many comic book incarnations

http://www.niehs.nih.gov/kids/lyrics/dreamer.htm – lyrics and a MIDI file for Foster's Beautiful Dreamer, as appropriated by the Joker